THE WORLD'S GREATEST
COLTS AND FILLIES
Poster Book

Voyageur Press

First published in 2008 by Voyageur Press, an imprint of MBI Publishing Company LLC, Galtier Plaza, Suite 200, 380 Jackson Street, St. Paul, MN 55101 USA

The information in this book is true and complete to the best of our knowledge. All recommendations are made without any guarantee on the part of the author or Publisher, who also disclaim any liability incurred in connection with the use of this data or specific details.

We recognize, further, that some words, model names, and designations mentioned herein are the property of the trademark holder. We use them for identification purposes only. This is not an official publication.

Voyageur Press titles are also available at discounts in bulk quantity for industrial or sales-promotional use. For details write to Special Sales Manager at MBI Publishing Company, Galtier Plaza, Suite 200, 380 Jackson Street, St. Paul, MN 55101 USA.

To find out more about our books, join us online at www.voyageurpress.com.

Library of Congress Cataloging-in-Publication Data

Johnson, Samantha.
  The world's greatest colts and fillies poster book / by Samantha Johnson ; photography by Daniel Johnson.
    p. cm.
  ISBN-13: 978-0-7603-3453-9 (softbound)
  1. Foals—Pictorial works. I. Johnson, Daniel, 1984–
II. Title.
SF303.J65 2008
636.1'070222—dc22

                                        2007043020

All photos are by Daniel Johnson.

About the author: Daniel Johnson specializes in equine photography, but he also enjoys photographing many other subjects, such as dogs, farm animals, gardens, and rural life. Dan also manages the family-owned horse farm and oversees the breeding, training, and showing of their horses. He lives in Phelps, Wisconsin.

Samantha Johnson is a certified horse show judge and a freelance writer. Her articles have appeared in many horse-centric magazines. She also works at Fox Hill Farm and specializes in foaling. She lives in Phelps, Wisconsin.

On the title pages: Daniel Johnson
On the cover: Daniel Johnson
On the back cover: Daniel Johnson

Editor: Amy Glaser
Designer: Brenda C. Canales

Printed in China

Gypsy Vanner Horses

Although the American registry for Gypsy Vanner horses was only recently established (1996), these horses have been bred as caravan horses in Great Britain for decades. They are rapidly gaining in popularity in the United States and are noted for their strength, friendly dispositions, trainability, and striking appearance. All colors and markings are acceptable, although many Gypsy Vanner horses are pinto.

Fun Fact

The Gypsy Vanner horse's heritage includes an influence from larger breeds, such as the Clydesdale, Friesian, and Shire. It is also influenced by native pony breeds, like the Dales pony.

Nursing

For the first three months of life, a foal's main source of nutrition comes from its mother's milk. Newborn foals nurse quite frequently, approximately five minutes every half an hour. The need for such constant nursing diminishes as the foal grows older and its daily fare is supplemented by grazing and eating hay or grain. By the time a foal is three months old, he nurses only every few hours or so. Foals are typically weaned between the ages of three and eight months.

Fun Fact
Once a foal has nursed for a few minutes, the mare often decides that "enough is enough," and she will gently nip the foal on its hindquarters, giving the signal that "time's up!"

Fly Control

All horses are somewhat agitated by pesky and bothersome flies, but foals seem to be particularly annoyed by bugs. At a very young age, they discover one of the easiest and best ways to keep the flies away—Mom's tail! Foals like to run underneath their dam's tail and drape it over their bodies or heads. This helps keep the flies from landing on their faces.

Fun Fact

While fly sprays are effective for older horses, most products are not safe for use on young foals, due to the heavy concentration of chemicals. This is why foals invent creative ways to keep the bugs at bay.

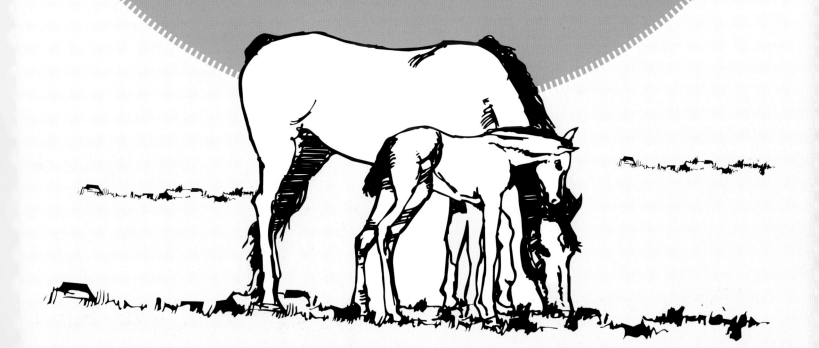

Itchy Foals

This two-week-old filly is attempting to scratch her ear with her hoof. At this age, foals still struggle with the basics of coordination, and many foals find it difficult to balance on three legs. With maturity, and with practice, their coordination improves.

Fun Fact

Foals are well known for being extremely itchy. In fact, one of the easiest ways to make friends with a shy foal is to scratch its neck or withers. Foals soon learn to associate people with the pleasantry of being scratched and begin to seek out their new human friends.

Busy as a Bee (or a Foal)

This five-week-old colt is just standing around—an unusual sight! Foals stay very busy most of the time and are rarely caught standing still. Between running and playing, exploring and grazing, nursing and napping, they find plenty to do and can keep themselves quite busy.

Fun Fact

Generally speaking, fillies are quieter and more subdued than colts. This is not to say that they don't enjoy running and playing, but colts tend to play harder and for longer periods of time. When foals get tired of playing games of running or chasing, they run back to the safety of their mothers and rest.

Water

Water is an extremely important part of a horse's daily diet. Adult horses drink several gallons of water each day. For the first few weeks of life, foals receive all of their hydration through nursing. Foals begin to experiment with taking sips of water when they are about a week old, and they begin drinking consistently after a couple of weeks. At this point, it is very important for foals to have access to a continual source of fresh water.

Fun Fact

Besides the importance of having water to drink, foals also use water for other purposes, such as playing. This foal is investigating a puddle of water after a rainstorm, testing out what it's like to have wet hooves and what happens when you splash too hard!

Rocky Mountain Horse

The Rocky Mountain horse has a history that traces back to the 1800s, but its official registry was not established until the late 1980s. Rocky Mountain horses are noted for their distinctive chocolate-colored coats with flaxen manes and tails, although not all Rocky Mountain horses exhibit this coloring.

Fun Fact

Although the breed's name implies they originated in the Rocky Mountains, the Rocky Mountain horse was actually developed in Kentucky. The name stems from the breed's foundation stallion, who was known as "The Rocky Mountain Horse" by equestrians in Kentucky.

Welsh Mountain Pony (Section A)

This foal is a Welsh Mountain pony, a breed that originated in the mountains of Wales. One of this foal's ancestors was imported from Wales in the 1970s, and this foal also descends from stock that was imported to the United States in the 1930s. The Welsh Mountain pony is an extremely beautiful breed, and they are popular as riding, driving, and children's ponies.

Fun Fact
Like many Welsh Mountain ponies, this mare and foal are chestnuts. Welsh Mountain ponies are also commonly grey, but they can be found in many other colors, including black, brown, bay, roan, buckskin, and palomino.

Black

This foal's coat is the color of a grey mouse. However, when she grows up, her coat will be completely black. Black horses are born this grey color, and when their foal coats shed out, a stunning black coat appears underneath. It is quite a transformation to watch!

Fun Fact

Black horses are very popular, partially because of their striking coloring, but also due in part to the enormous popularity of the classic children's horse books, such as Black Beauty *by Anna Sewell and* The Black Stallion *by Walter Farley. Many children dream of having a black horse of their very own.*

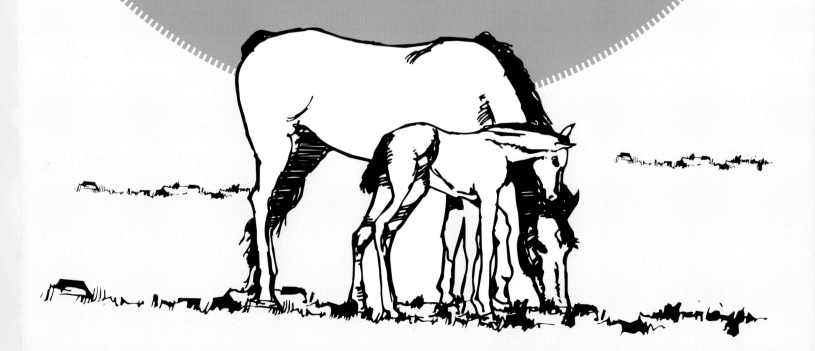

Are You My Mother?

When mares and foals are kept together in herds, it is very interesting to watch them interact. This Morgan foal is approaching a mare that is not his mother. The reaction of the mare will depend on her temperament. Most mares will ignore the foal's curiosity and allow him to stay with them, however a cranky mare may chase the little intruder away, perhaps pinning her ears or attempting to bite him.

Fun Fact

Although a mare and foal can recognize one another by sight, they usually rely on their sense of smell to recognize each other. That's why if a mare and her foal have been separated (even for a short time), you will notice the mare sniffing her foal when they are reunited. This is how she convinces herself that it really is her baby.

Palomino

A palomino horse is a glorious sight to behold. In fact, it is one of the most popular and sought-after horse colors. And why not? Their coats sparkle like gold and their pure white manes and tails contrast beautifully against the golden luster of their bodies, a combination that is very pleasing to the eye.

Fun Fact
This young palomino filly is still sporting her baby coat, which is a pale cream color. When this baby coat sheds out, the true golden coloring of her palomino coat will shine through.

Say Cheese!
(Or, Rather, Say Grass!)

While it looks as though this filly is smiling for the camera, she's actually displaying a reflex known as the Flehmen response. When a horse encounters a smell that seems foreign or strange, it will often raise its upper lip and flex its neck into the air.

Fun Fact

Many other mammals, including cats, giraffes, llamas, and buffalo, also display the Flehmen response. It is not strictly limited to equines, although it is most commonly thought of as an equine reflex.

Norwegian Fjord

As the name implies, the Norwegian Fjord horse originated in Norway, and its most distinguishable characteristic is its dun coloring. Norwegian Fjords are noted for being hardy animals and are often used today as driving horses. Although they are referred to as horses, they often stay pony size (under 14.2 hands).

Fun Fact

Although the Norwegian Fjord filly in this photo appears to be a palomino, she is actually a dun Norwegian Fjord, and her baby coat is disguising the darker hair that will later become more apparent.

Pinto

While many foals are solid-colored with only a few white markings on their legs or faces, some foals have more extensive white markings that intermix with their main body color. This is known as pinto coloring, although there are also more specific terms that describe the exact type of white markings, such as tobiano, overo, or sabino.

Fun Fact

Historically, black-and-white horses were known as piebalds, while any other color-and-white horses were known as skewbalds. These quaint terms are now considered old-fashioned, since we now have specific terminology to use when describing these types of coloring.

Morgan

Morgan horses are very popular for their versatility and useful size, usually between 14.2 and 15.2 hands. The exact origin of the Morgan horse is unknown, although some sources believe they descend from Welsh Cobs.

Fun Fact

The most famous Morgan horse is undoubtedly the breed's foundation stallion, Justin Morgan. Marguerite Henry, beloved author of children's horse stories, dedicated an entire book to this famous Morgan, Justin Morgan Had a Horse.

Halter Training

Even though it will be years before this foal will be trained to ride or drive, his training has already begun. The first type of training that a foal encounters is halter training. Foals are usually introduced to being haltered and led when they are a few days old. At first they resist the idea of having to wear a halter, and they usually don't like the idea of having to walk along next to their handler. However, patience pays off and by the time a foal is two or three weeks old, it is very good about being haltered and led.

Fun Fact

Foals should never be turned out to pasture while it is wearing a halter. For safety purposes, the halter should always be removed before the foal is turned loose to play.`

Let's Be Friends?

These six-week-old foals are getting acquainted for the first time. Foals are often very shy around other horses and usually stay quite close to their mothers for the first few weeks of life. Once their initial shyness begins to wear off, they start to become bolder and begin to approach one another. Even still, it will probably be another week or two before these two foals begin playing together.

Fun Fact

Even if these foals weren't shy, they probably still wouldn't be allowed to play together for the first few weeks. Their mothers would see to that! Mares are very protective of their foals and usually keep them quite close until they are about a month old.

Whiskers

Whiskers are a very important characteristic of foals. In addition to being oh-so-cute, whiskers serve a practical purpose. When a new foal is born, it must begin nursing right away. The long whiskers on the muzzle help them to easily locate their mother's udder so that they can begin nursing. Whiskers are also very helpful while a foal is learning about the world because they prevent them from bumping into things while they explore.

Fun Fact

A newborn foal has additional whiskers on the end of its nose, but these disappear after the first few days. The regular long whiskers on the sides of the muzzle remain, as do the long hairs on the bottom of the chin.

Bay

This reddish-colored colt might look chestnut, but he is actually a bay. Bays are a darker, deeper shade of reddish-brown (as opposed to chestnuts, which are reddish-orange), accompanied by black "points" (manes, tails, ear tips, and legs), which chestnuts do not have.

Fun Fact

This young colt is only a few weeks old, so his adult coat color has not yet fully developed. As he matures, his ear tips will darken, the light hair on his legs will shed out to black, and his mane and tail will become entirely black.

Taking Care of Foals

Like all mammals, foals need a lot of rest and frequent meals of milk. However, foals also need other types of special care. Foals need to be regularly dewormed to protect them against parasites, their hooves must be regularly trimmed by a knowledgable farrier, and they need to be examined by a veterinarian at birth to verify that they are healthy and strong.

Fun Fact

Some breeders like to imprint their foals, which means that they try to introduce their foals to many different objects and sensations from the moment they are born. These breeders feel that it helps their foals to be less intimidated and frightened by new objects later on.

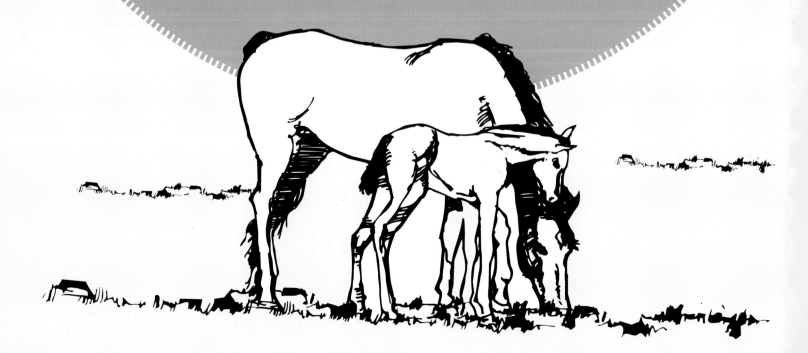

Curious Foals

Foals are well known for their irresistible cuteness, adorable antics, and insatiable curiosity. They are eager to explore everything about the world, from rocks to sand to flowers to fence posts.

Fun Fact

Foals have plenty of time for exploring things because they aren't busy with grazing until they are at least a month old. Until they begin grazing, they don't have much to occupy their time except for napping, so they spend many hours exploring and checking out the world.

Newborns

This pony mare has just delivered a brand-new chestnut filly. Foals learn to stand within the first hour of life, and this foal has just managed to stand on her wobbly legs. Now she is focusing on her next important task: nursing! A foal must drink from its mother's udder within the first two hours after being born. The first milk that the foal drinks is called colostrum, and it is a very important type of milk that helps to protect a foal from illness.

Fun Fact

After the first successful drink of milk, a newborn foal usually becomes very sleepy and will quickly fall to sleep. This nap is usually very short, after which time the foal immediately begins looking for more milk to drink!

Child's Pony

This young foal has a very important career ahead of her. When she is old enough, she will be trained to be a child's riding pony. Because she will only be 12 hands when she is fully grown, she will be the perfect size for a child to ride. However, before she will be ready to help a child learn to ride, she will need many months of training herself.

Fun Fact

When a horse trainer is evaluating a young horse or pony as a potential child's pony, one of the most important characteristics is the animal's temperament. To be suitable for a child to ride, the horse or pony must be quiet, sensible, easygoing, and not easily frightened.

Give Me a "Hand"

Horses are measured in "hands," which is a term traditionally used by horsemen to refer to 4 inches. Therefore, if a pony is 10 hands, then he is 40 inches tall. A 15-hand horse is 60 inches tall. A 13.2-hand pony is 54 inches tall (13 hands x 4 inches = 52 inches + 2 inches = 54 inches).

Fun Fact

A horse's height is measured at the highest point of its withers. To accurately measure a horse, you must use an official measuring stick, which will give a much more precise reading than some of the other methods of measuring.

Roan

At first glance, this colt appears to be black, or is he grey? Actually, he's a roan, which means that he has white hairs intermixed within his coat. While roan is not actually a color, it is a modifying gene that alters a horse's coat. The color of a roan horse's coat will change with the seasons, going from very dark to very light and then settling to a medium shade for the majority of the year.

Fun Fact

The white hairs in a roan horse's coat are usually the most numerous on the hindquarters and midsection. There are fewer white hairs on the neck and shoulders and very few white hairs on the face and legs.

Growing Up

These foals are now two months old and are becoming much more independent. By the time they are this age, they are spending less time with their mothers and more time playing and exploring the world.

Fun Fact

This two-month-old grey filly is spending all of her time with the black filly and her mother. She even tries to nurse from the black filly's mother so that she won't have to bother going back to her own mother, who seems to like the foal care arrangements!

White Markings

You may notice that foals have different sizes of white markings on their faces, ranging from a small star to a narrow stripe and all the way up to a large blaze. This filly's face has a very wide blaze that extends all the way down to her nostrils.

Fun Fact

Researchers have discovered that white markings on the face usually go along with white markings on the legs. For instance, a foal with a tiny star might only have a short sock on one foot, whereas a foal with a narrow stripe might have white stockings on two legs. This filly's wide blaze is accompanied by high white stockings on all four of her legs.

Tobiano

This foal exhibits the tobiano color pattern found on pinto horses. There are several characteristics that signify the coat pattern is of the tobiano variety, including four white legs accompanied by its vertical white body markings. Another important characteristic is that tobianos typically have moderately marked faces.

Fun Fact

If a horse inherits two copies of the tobiano gene (one from each parent), then the horse is said to be homozygous tobiano, which means that every one of that horse's offspring will possess the tobiano pattern.

Dales Pony

This black foal is a Dales pony. The Dales is a native pony breed from the United Kingdom, known for its strength and stamina. Dales ponies were used as farm horses in England and are popular today for riding and driving. They usually stand 14 to 14.2 hands and are most often found in dark colors (black, bay, or brown), although the occasional grey or roan is also seen. Dales ponies have minimal white markings.

Fun Fact

Dales ponies are registered as Section A or Section B, depending on the amount of white marking they possess. Section A denotes appropriate white markings that are within the ideal parameters set by the Dales Pony Society, while Section B is for animals with more white markings than desired.

Mutual Grooming

These two foals have discovered something very nice about having a friend. When a foal has a friend that is the same size, the friend can help scratch those itchy places that the foal cannot reach. You will often see two foals "mutually grooming" each other, which means that they scratch each other's withers or neck with their teeth, or you may see them engaging in face play, as these two colts.

Fun Fact

Sometimes you will see mutual grooming between a mare and her foal, but this is not as common as two young horses grooming each other. This may be because foals are itchy, or it could be because mares are more engrossed with other tasks like grazing.

Grey

This adorable foal is 3 months old, and her coat is very black. It might surprise you to know that she's truly a grey horse. As she grows older, her coat will continue to become lighter until she is completely white. It's hard to imagine such a black foal becoming a white adult horse, but grey coloring uniquely affects a horse's coat.

Fun Fact

Not all grey horses are born black, although many people mistakenly believe so. Grey horses can be born any color: bay, chestnut, palomino, buckskin, black, and even spotted!

Feathers

Feathers are not just for birds. Some breeds of horses have them, too. On a horse, the long silky hairs above the hoof (hanging from the fetlock) are called feathers. Some breeds are well known for their abundant feathering, while other breeds have little or none. However, in many breeds, the feathers are shaved off so that the fetlocks are smooth.

Fun Fact

This foal, a Gypsy Vanner, is an example of a breed that is well known for its heavy feathering. Other breeds that are noted for abundant feathering include the Welsh Cob, the Shire, the Clydesdale, and other draft breeds.

Conformation

It can be very difficult to properly judge a foal's conformation because it is continually growing and changing. Foals don't always grow at the same rate in different parts of their body. Sometimes foals go through periods where they look unbalanced, but as they keep growing, this usually resolves itself.

Fun Fact
Many breeders go by the philosophy that foals should be evaluated at 3 weeks, 3 months, and 3 years, and if you like what you see at those points, it doesn't really matter what phases the foal goes through in between those points of time.

"Fjun" with Fjords

At first glance, you might think that all Norwegian Fjords are dun colored. While this is true, there are actually several shades of dun coloring in the Norwegian Fjords, ranging from yellow to grey to white. Each color has its own name, including brunblakk, kvit, ful, rodblakk, gra, and ulsblakk.

Fun Fact
Did you know that the black stripe down the middle of a Norwegian Fjord's mane is called a midtstol and that the black stripe down the middle of the tail is called a halefjaer?

Eyes

Most adult horses have brown eyes, although you will occasionally see an adult horse with blue eyes, such as a cremello or a horse that has a wide blaze that extends over the eyes. Foals often have blue eyes at birth that will later darken to brown.

Fun Fact

Foals that are one of the dilute colors, such as palomino, buckskin, smoky black, or cremello, sometimes have amber eyes. This is a unique shade that actually appears transparent at times and makes them very special!

Gaits

This six-week-old colt is cantering, a fast, three-beat gait. Even faster than cantering is galloping, a four-beat gait. This is the gait used by horses during a horse race. Slower than the canter or gallop is the two-beat trot, and the slowest gait of all is the walk, a four-beat gait.

Fun Fact

Some foals show an early preference for cantering and always seem to be either walking or cantering. Other foals are fond of the trot and rarely bother with cantering. It's interesting to watch a foal's preferences of which gait it likes best.

Colts & Fillies

All baby horses are called foals. Male foals are called colts, and female foals are called fillies. They are typically known by these names until they are approximately three years old, at which time colts become stallions and fillies become mares.

Fun Fact

Some people incorrectly refer to all foals as colts, which can be misleading. The term "colt" should only be used when referring to a male horse under the age of three. A female foal should never be referred to as a colt but should always be called a filly.

Registration

Owners of foals that are eligible for registration within their breed's society must apply for registration. This usually means that the owner must fill out an application that lists the foal's sire, dam, date of birth, color, and markings. In addition, the owner must fill out a diagram that illustrates the placement of the foal's markings. Photos must also be provided to verify the color and markings.

Fun Fact

Because this filly is palomino and has very pale legs, it's hard to tell where the white stockings on her legs are. In order to take registration photos, her owner will have to wet down the filly's legs so that the white markings become visible.

My, What (Little) Teeth You Have!

Ooohh, look, she's grazing. Or is she? This newborn filly is two days old. While she is mimicking her mother and going through the motions of grazing, nothing is really happening because the filly has no teeth! Because foals like to copy everything that they see other horses doing, they practice grazing before they are physically able to do so.

Fun Fact

A foal's first teeth appear at about one week of age, with the four central incisors appearing first. Foals eventually have 24 deciduous (baby) teeth, which fall out and are later replaced by 40 or 42 permanent teeth by the time the horse is five years old.

Welsh Pony of Cob Type (Section C)

Larger than a Welsh Mountain pony (Section A) and smaller than a Welsh Cob (Section D), the Welsh pony of Cob Type (Section C) is a substantial pony and stands up to 13.2 hands. Section C ponies are athletic and talented equines with strength and stamina. Welsh Section C ponies are excellent in many disciplines, including driving, jumping, English, and Western classes.

Fun Fact

This young Section C colt is pictured with his 12-hand Welsh Mountain pony (Section A) dam. His sire is a 14.2-hand Welsh Cob (Section D). Because this colt will mature at around 13 hands, he will be as tall as his dam by the time he is six months old!

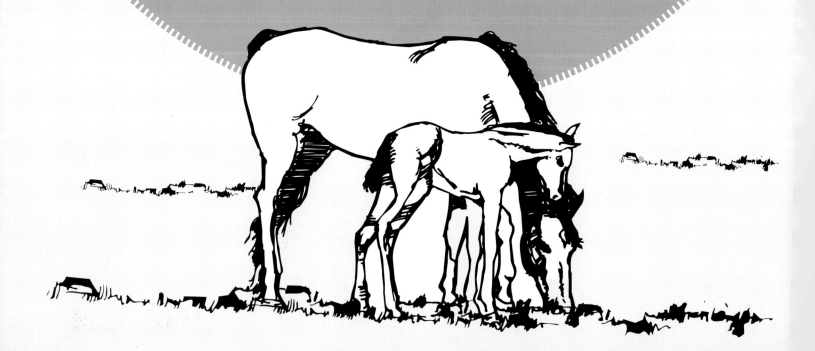

Driving Pony

Although you wouldn't know it by looking at this young foal, he has a very big future ahead of him. As soon as he is old enough, this colt will begin his training to become a driving pony. This means that he will wear a driving harness and be hitched to a small wagon or cart. Many horses and ponies are trained to drive, as this is a very popular discipline among horse owners.

Fun Fact

There are many different types of driving, including carriage, pleasure, draft, combined, fine-harness, and roadster. Some horse owners focus on one particular type of driving, while other owners dabble in all of the different possibilities.

British Native Ponies

Several pony breeds originated in the United Kingdom and are known as British Native ponies. Some of the breeds include Connemara, Highland, Dales, Fell, Dartmoor, Exmoor, Shetland, and all four sections of Welsh ponies and Cobs. These breeds are very popular in the United Kingdom, and many are gaining interest in the United States.

Fun Fact

This young Welsh pony is an wonderful example of the qualities that the British Native pony breeds are known for. He exhibits hardiness, pony character, and good type and bone. His parents were imported from the United Kingdom.

Chestnut

The color of this reddish-orange filly is called chestnut. Unlike bays, which are dark red or brown with black legs, chestnuts have legs that are the same color as their bodies, a deep orange or light red. Their manes and tails can be flaxen (pale cream or white) or red. Chestnuts with red manes and tails are sometimes called sorrels.

Fun Fact

If a foal's sire (father) is a chestnut and its dam (mother) is a chestnut, then the foal will be a chestnut. Chestnut bred to chestnut always results in a chestnut foal. This is because chestnut is a recessive gene, similar to blue eyes in humans.